FOR JOHN "SPARKY" JOHNSON

CHAPTERS

George Beard and
Harold Hutchins
present:
A "Deny Everything"
Production

EPISODE 1
the Fantom
Principal

A Long time Ago, in a
Elementary School far
far away...

There were two
cool kids named
George and Harold.

We rule

Me too

They had a evil
Principle Named
Mr. Krupp, who was
strong in
the ways
of the
FORSE!

Blah
Blah

He FORSED
Them to Study
Blah Blah Blah

He FORSED
Them to Clean
Blah
Blah
Blah

And he FORSED
Them to
BEHAVE!
HA HA
HA!

So George and Harold Hipnotised Him.

You will obey our every command!

OK.

SNAP!

You are now "Captain Underpants"

OK

HA HA HA

It started out as a Joke, but it wasent funny for long!

HA HA HA

Tra-La-Laaa

Hey

Come Back

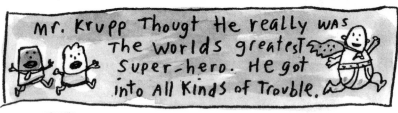

Mr. Krupp Thougt He really was the worlds greatest super-hero. He got into all kinds of Trouble.

George and Harold had to save him (and the entire planet)...

...Twice!

NoW The oNLy way they cAN Turn cAptain Under-pants back into MR. krupp, is To pour water over his head!

BuT The worst Part is That Geo-rge and Harold Have To keep An eye on mr. Krupp.

Blah Blah Blah

Because For Some **STRANGE** reason, whenever he hears sombody Snap There fingers...

← SNAP!

... he TurNs BACK into You-KNow-Who!

TRA LA LAAA

So whatever you Do, **PLEASE DON'T** SNAP Your fingers Around Mr. Krupp.

You heard the man! **PLEASE PLEASE, PLEASE** DoN't SNAP Those fingers!

This has been A public servise Anouncement from George and Harold... who **STILL** Deny every Thing!

CHAPTER 1
GEORGE AND HAROLD

This is George Beard and Harold Hutchins.
George is the kid on the left with the tie
and the flat-top. Harold is the one on the
right with the T-shirt and the bad haircut.
Remember that now.

If you were looking for a few words to describe George and Harold, you might come up with *kind*, *funny*, *smart*, *determined*, and *deep*.

Just ask their principal, Mr. Krupp. He'll tell you that George and Harold are **KIND**a **FUNNY**-lookin' **SMART** alecks who are **DETERMINED** to drive everybody off the **DEEP** end!

But don't listen to him.

George and Harold are actually very clever and good-hearted boys. Their only problem is that they're fourth graders. And at George and Harold's school, fourth graders are expected to sit still and pay attention for *seven hours a day*!

George and Harold are just not very good at that.

The only thing George and Harold *are* good at is being silly. Unfortunately, George and Harold's silliness gets them into trouble every now and then. Sometimes it gets them into a LOT of trouble. And one time it got them into *SO MUCH* trouble, it almost caused the entire Earth to be destroyed by an army of giant evil zombie nerds!

But before I can tell you that story, I have to tell you *this* story....

CHAPTER 2

THE EVIL SPACE GUYS

One dark, clear night in Piqua, Ohio,
a flaming object was seen streaking across
the quiet midnight sky.

It shone brightly for a second or two,
then fizzled out just above Jerome Horwitz
Elementary School. Nobody gave it a
second thought.

The next day, everything seemed pretty normal. Nobody noticed anything different about the school. Nobody paid any attention to the roof. And of course, nobody looked up and said, "Hey, what's that big spaceship thingy doing on the roof of the school?"

Perhaps if they had, the horrible ordeal that followed might never have happened, and you wouldn't be sitting here reading about it right now. But they didn't, it did, and, well, here we are.

As we can all plainly see, there was a spaceship on top of the building. And inside that spaceship were three of the most evil, hideous, and merciless space-men ever to set foot on the roof of a small midwestern elementary school.

Their names were Zorx, Klax, and Jennifer. Their mission? To take over planet Earth.

"First," said Zorx, "we must find a way to infiltrate the school."

"Then," said Klax, "we will turn all the children into giant, super-powered evil zombie nerds!"

"Finally," said Jennifer, "we will use them to take over the world!"

Zorx and Klax laughed and laughed.

"Silence, you fools!" barked Jennifer. "If our plan is to work, we must wait until it is narratively convenient. In the meantime, we will watch their every move on our trinocloscope!"

CHAPTER 3

FUN WITH SCIENCE

Early that same morning, George and Harold were sitting in their 10:15 AM science class making silly noises.

"Meeowwwww," George mewed softly, without moving his lips.

"Rrrr-rrr-rrrr," growled Harold, without opening his mouth.

"There it is *again*!" exclaimed their science teacher, Mr Fyde. "I *distinctly* heard a cat and a dog in here!"

"We didn't hear anything," the children said, trying not to laugh.

"I-I must be *hearing* things again," Mr Fyde worried.

"Maybe you should leave and go and see a doctor," said George with concern.

"I can't," said Mr Fyde. "Today is the day of the big *volcano experiment*."

The children all groaned. Mr Fyde's science experiments were usually the most idiotic things on earth. They almost never worked, and were *always* boring.

But today's experiment was different. Mr Fyde brought in a large, fake-looking volcano that he had made out of papier-mâché. He filled the volcano with a box of ordinary baking soda.

"Baking soda is also called 'sodium bicarbonate,'" explained Mr Fyde.

"Meeeeowwwwwww."

"Umm…" said Mr Fyde, "did any of you children just hear – umm, uh … never mind."

Mr Fyde opened up a bottle of clear liquid. "Now watch what happens when I pour vinegar into the baking soda," he said.

The children watched as the tiny volcano started to rumble. Soon, a large glob of foamy goop spurted out the top. The goop poured over the desk and dripped onto the floor, creating a huge mess.

"Oops," said Mr Fyde. "I guess I used too much baking soda."

George and Harold were stunned.

"How did you do that?" asked Harold.

"Well," said Mr Fyde, "the vinegar acts as a liberating agent, which releases the gaseous carbonate radical element of the sodium bicarbo—"

"Meeeeooowwwwwwwww."

"Umm … uh," Mr Fyde paused. "Uh, e-excuse me, children. I-I've got to go and see a doctor."

Mr Fyde put on his coat and hurried through the door. George and Harold got up and studied the messy volcano experiment with great interest.

"Are you thinking what I'm thinking?" asked George.

"I think I'm thinking what you're thinking," said Harold.

CHAPTER 4
THE SETUP

After school, the two boys raced to George's house and got down to business.

George and Harold sat down and began creating a fake cupcake recipe.

"We'll just add a box of baking soda and a bottle of vinegar to this recipe," said George. "And whoever makes these cupcakes will get a big surprise!"

"Let's add *two* boxes of baking soda and *two* bottles of vinegar to the recipe," said Harold. "That way, they'll get an even *bigger* surprise!"

"Good idea!" laughed George.

CHAPTER 5

MR. KRUPP'S KRISPY KRUPCAKES

The next morning at school, George and Harold strolled into the cafeteria and taped a festive-looking card to the kitchen door.

Soon the lunch ladies arrived.

"Oh, look," said Miss Creant, the head lunch lady. "Today is Mr Krupp's birthday and he'd like us to make a batch of cupcakes just for him! Isn't that cute?"

"I've got an idea," said the cook, Mrs DePoint. "Why don't we surprise him and make cupcakes for the *whole school*!"

"Good thinking," said Miss Creant. "Let's see now…this recipe serves 10, and we have about 1,000 students and faculty in the school, so…

…we'll need 100 eggs, 150 cups of flour, 200 boxes of baking soda, 7 quarts of green food colouring, 50 sticks of butter, 150 cups of sugar – and, let's see… Oh yes, 200 bottles of *vinegar*!"

MR. KRUPP'S KRISPY KRUPCAKES

INGREDIENTS

1 egg
1½ cups of Flour
2 Boxes Baking Soda
½ cups Sugar
½ Stick Butter
Green Food Coloring
2 Bottles Vinegar

MAKES 10 CUPCAKES

DIRECTIONS

Mix Flour and Sugar with baking soda, and egg. Melt butter, pour into mixture. Stir in Food coloring. Now Add Vinegar. Mix well. Pour into cupcake Thingies. Bake At 45 degrees For 3 hours.

The lunch ladies scurried about, gathering everything they needed. They dumped the eggs, food colouring, milk, and baking soda into a large vat and began to mix thoroughly.

Then somebody poured in the vinegar...

CHAPTER 6
WHAT HAPPENED NEXT

(Note: Please shake this book back and forth uncontrollably when you read the following word. Also, shout it out as loud as you can. Don't worry, you won't get in trouble.)

"KA-BLOOOOOSH!"

CHAPTER 6 ½

HERE COMES THE GOOP!

A giant wave of green goop crashed through the cafeteria doors and splashed down the halls, swallowing everything in its path. Book bags, bulletin boards, lunch boxes, coat racks, trophy cases...nothing could stand in the way of the gigantic green glob o' goo.

It travelled down the north, east, and west wings of the school, covering everything from the drinking fountains to the text on this page. It squished into lockers, and squashed down the stairs. It billowed in_____ ___and ballowe___

It wasn't long before the green goop
began spilling into all the classrooms.

"Uh-oh," said George. "Something tells
me the lunch ladies made more than just
one batch of Mr Krupp's Krispy Krupcakes."

"But – but that was *their* idea, not
ours," cried Harold.

"Speaking of *ideas*," said George, "I've
got a good one."

"What?" asked Harold.

"RUN!" cried George.

CHAPTER 7

THE WRATH OF THE CAFETERIA LADIES

The next afternoon, as cleaning crews sorted through the sticky green hallways and sticky green classrooms, the cafeteria ladies had a meeting with Mr Krupp in his sticky green office.

"But it wasn't even my birthday!" cried Mr Krupp.

"We know you had nothing to do with this!" said Miss Creant. "We think it was those two awful boys, George and Harold!"

"Well, *duh!*" said Mr Krupp, rolling his eyes. "OF COURSE IT WAS GEORGE AND HAROLD!!! But do you have any proof?"

"PROOF?!!?" said the lunch ladies. "Why, George and Harold are *always* playing tricks on us! Every day, they change the letters around on our lunch sign. They put pepper in the napkin dispensers and unscrew the caps on the saltshakers... They start food fights... They go sledging on our lunch trays... They make everybody laugh so the milk squirts out their noses... And they're *constantly creating these awful comic books about us*!!!"

CHAPTER 8

CAPTAIN UNDERPANTS AND THE NIGHT OF THE LIVING LUNCH LADIES

By George Beard
and Harold Hutchins.

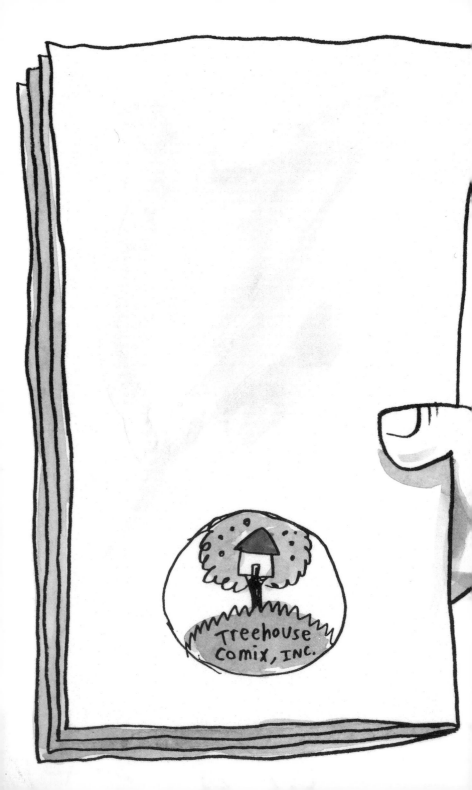

CHAPTER 9
QUITTIN' TIME

"We're *fed up* with those two boys!" cried Miss Creant. "They're always making fun of our cooking!"

"Yeah!" said Mrs DePoint. "Our food isn't *that* bad. I ate here once and hardly got sick at all!"

"Well, I can't punish them if we don't have any proof," said Mr Krupp.

"Fine!" said the lunch ladies. "Then we *quit*!"

"Ladies, ladies," cried Mr Krupp. "Be reasonable! You can't just *quit* on such short notice."

But the lunch ladies didn't care. They marched right out of Mr Krupp's sticky green office, and that was the end of that.

"Rats!" cried Mr Krupp. "Now where am I going to find three new lunch ladies by tomorrow morning?"

Suddenly there was a knock on Mr Krupp's door. Three very large women wearing *lots* of makeup walked into his office.

"Hello," said the first woman. "My name is, uh, Zorx*ette*. These are my, uh, sisters, *Klaxette* and, umm, *Jenniferette*. We've come to apply for jobs as cafeteria ladies."

"Wow," said Mr Krupp. "Do you have any experience?"

"No," said Klaxette.

"Do you have any credentials?" asked Mr Krupp.

"No," said Zorxette.

"Do you have any references?" asked Mr Krupp.

"No," said Jenniferette.

"You're hired!" said Mr Krupp.

"Wonderful," said Jenniferette. "Now our plan to take over the world is – er, I mean, our plan to *feed the children healthy, nutritional meals* is underway!"

The three new lunch ladies laughed horribly. Then they left Mr Krupp's office and got started preparing the next day's lunch menu.

"Well, *that* was easy," said Mr Krupp.
"Now to take care of George and Harold!"

CHAPTER 10

BUSTED!

George and Harold were in study hall when they heard the dreaded announcement over the intercom:

> "George Beard and Harold Hutchins, please report to Mr. Krupp's office immediately."

"Oh, no," cried Harold. "We're busted!"
"No way!" said George. "Remember, what happened yesterday was *not our fault*! We didn't do it – it was an *accident*!"

But Mr. Krupp was not as understanding. "I can't prove it, but I *know* you boys are responsible for yesterday's disaster," Mr Krupp said. "I'm going to punish you by taking away your cafeteria privileges for the rest of the year! *No more cafeteria food for you two!*"

"No more cafeteria food?" whispered Harold. "I thought he said he was going to *punish* us."

"Yeah." George smiled. "Maybe if we're *really* bad, he'll take away our *homework* privileges, too!"

"I heard that!" screamed Mr Krupp. "From now on, you boys are going to have to pack your own lunches and eat them in my office so I can keep an eye on you!"

"Rats!" said Harold.

"But we didn't do it!" George protested. "WE DIDN'T DO IT!"

"Too bad!" said Mr Krupp.

"Boy," said George. "This is probably the first time we've got in trouble for something we *didn't* do."

"Unless you count all those times we didn't do our homework," said Harold.

"Oh, yeah," laughed George.

CHAPTER 11

BROWN BAGGIN' IT

The next day, George and Harold each
brought their own sandwiches to Mr
Krupp's office for lunch.

"I'll trade you half of my peanut-butter-
and-gummy-worm sandwich," said George,
"for half of your tuna-salad-with-chocolate-
chips-and-miniature-marshmallows
sandwich."

"Sure," said Harold. "Y'want some
barbecue sauce on that?"

"You kids are DISGUSTING!" Mr Krupp
shouted.

Soon George and Harold were munching on potato chips with whipped cream and chocolate sprinkles. Mr Krupp was turning green.

"What's for dessert?" asked Harold.

"Hard-boiled eggs dipped in hot fudge and Skittles!" said George.

"AAAUGH!" screamed Mr Krupp. *I can't stand it any more!* He got up and stumbled out the door for some fresh air.

"You know," said George. "Now that Mr Krupp is gone, we could run to the cafeteria and change the letters around on the lunch sign."

"Cool," said Harold.

So George and Harold sneaked to the cafeteria. But when they read the lunch sign, they were a bit confused.

"What's going on here?" said George.

"It looks like somebody's already changed the sign," said Harold.

"Forget the sign," said George. "Look at everybody! *They've* changed!"

It was true. All the kids and teachers in school were entering the cafeteria looking as normal as ever. But they were leaving the cafeteria looking quite different.

"Look!" cried George. "They're all wearing broken eyeglasses held together with masking tape . . . and they've all got vinyl pocket protectors!!! They've all turned into—"

"Nerds!" Harold gasped.

"And look at their skin," said George. "They're all grey and clammy. This can only mean one thing!"

"They're – they're ZOMBIE nerds?!!?" asked Harold.

"I'm afraid so," said George.

"Let's just hope they're friendly!" said Harold.

"Whoever heard of a *friendly* zombie nerd?" asked George.

"I'm afraid," Harold whined.

"There's no time to be afraid," said George. "We've got to get to the bottom of this!"

"*That's* what I'm afraid of," said Harold.

CHAPTER 12
THE BOTTOM OF THIS

George and Harold crawled into the cafeteria and sneaked through the kitchen doors. There they hid behind a table while the incredibly naughty cafeteria ladies from outer space discussed their plans to take over the world.

"Look at those puny earthlings!" laughed Zorx. "They're all drinking EVIL ZOMBIE NERD MILKSHAKES and transforming before our very eyes!"

"It won't be long now," said Klax. "Tomorrow, we'll feed them SUPER EVIL RAPID-GROWTH JUICE! Then they will grow to the size of Xleqxisfp trees."

"Exactly," sneered Jennifer. "Then we will unleash our giant evil zombie nerds upon the earth, and soon the planet will be OURS!"

The three evil space guys threw back their heads and laughed hysterically.

"We've got to tell Mr Krupp about this," Harold whispered.

"Right," whispered George. "But first, we've got to get rid of that SUPER EVIL RAPID-GROWTH JUICE!"

George carefully reached up and swiped the carton of juice.

"What should we do with it?" asked Harold.

"Let's pour it out the window," said George. "That way it won't do any damage."

"Good idea," said Harold.

While the naughty cafeteria ladies
continued laughing, George quietly
emptied the carton of SUPER EVIL RAPID-
GROWTH JUICE out the window.

"You know," whispered Harold, "Mr
Krupp is never going to believe that
sinister cafeteria ladies from outer space
have turned everybody into evil zombie
nerds."

"Sure he'll believe us – he's **GOT** to
believe us!" said George. "I *hope* he believes
us!"

CHAPTER 13

HE DOESN'T BELIEVE THEM

"That's the most *ridiculous* story I've ever heard!" laughed Mr Krupp.

"But it's true!" cried Harold.

"Yeah," said George. "Everybody in the entire school is an evil zombie nerd! The kids, the teachers…*everybody*!"

"All right," said Mr Krupp. "I'll prove it to you!" He pressed the button on his intercom and called for his secretary.

Soon Miss Anthrope entered the room. She was dressed in a pink polka-dot polyester dress, with orthopedic knee-high stockings and ugly brown arch-support loafers.

"See?" said Harold. "She's dressed like a *nerd*!"

"She always dresses like that," snapped Mr Krupp.

"But she's grey and clammy and reeks of *freakish zombified death*!" cried George.

"She *always smells like that*!" Mr Krupp argued. "And she's always grey and clammy, too!"

George and Harold had to admit that school secretaries were not very good subjects to compare and contrast with evil zombie nerds.

But then, Miss Anthrope leaned over and took a huge bite out of Mr. Krupp's desk. *"Must destroy Earth,"* she moaned as she took another bite.

Even Mr Krupp had to agree that Miss Anthrope was acting a bit more evil than usual.

So George and Harold took Mr Krupp down to the cafeteria to confront the evil lunch ladies.

Suddenly, out of the shadows stepped the evil Zorx. "Gotcha!" Zorx cried, as he grabbed on to Harold's shoulders.

"Aaaagh!" screamed Harold. He squirmed away, pulling Zorx's gloves off and revealing two slimy green tentacles.

"See, Mr Krupp?" said George. "We told you they were space guys!"

"You FOOLS!" screamed Zorx. "Now we will destroy you!" The evil Zorx pointed his tentacle at George, Harold, and Mr Krupp, and snapped his fingers:

"SNAP!"

Suddenly, Mr Krupp began to change.

A heroic grin spread across Mr Krupp's face. He threw out his chest and placed his fists firmly at his sides, looking quite triumphant.

"Uh-oh," said George. "That evil space guy just snapped his fingers! Now Mr Krupp is turning into *you-know-who*!"

"Hey, wait a second," said Harold. "Tentacles don't have fingers! You can't *snap* a tentacle!"

"There's no time to argue the physical improbabilities of this story," said George. "We've got to stop Mr Krupp from changing into Captain Underpants before it's too late!"

CHAPTER 14
IT'S TOO LATE

Mr Krupp turned and dashed out the door. His clothes flew off behind him as the hallways echoed with jubilant proclamations about the superiority of underwear.

George and Harold dashed after him, but the door was quickly blocked by Zorx, Klax, and Jennifer.

"You wanna get out of this kitchen," the evil Jennifer mocked, "you gotta go through *US*!"

George grabbed a rolling pin. Harold grabbed a cast-iron frying pan.

"I sure hope we don't have to resort to incredibly graphic violence," said Harold.

"Me, too," said George.

CHAPTER 15

THE INCREDIBLY GRAPHIC VIOLENCE CHAPTER, PART 1 (IN FLIP-O-RAMA™)

WARNING:

The following chapter contains terribly inappropriate scenes that certainly do not belong in a children's book.

If you are offended by such senselessness, please put this book down immediately, raise your arms over your head, and run screaming to your nearest shoe shop. When you get there, ask them to make you a cheeseburger.

(Note: This probably won't help you a bit, but we think it will be funny.)

PILKEY® BRAND

D-RAMA

HERE'S HOW IT WORKS!

STEP 1

Place your *left* hand inside the dotted lines marked "LEFT HAND HERE." Hold the book open *flat*.

STEP 2

Grasp the *right-hand* page with your right thumb and index finger (inside the dotted lines marked "RIGHT THUMB HERE").

STEP 3

Now *quickly* flip the right-hand page back and forth until the picture appears to be *animated*.

(For extra fun, try adding your own sound-effects!)

FLIP-O-RAMA 1

(pages 79 and 81)

Remember, flip *only* page 79.
While you are flipping, be sure you
can see the picture on page 79
and the one on page 81.
If you flip quickly, the two
pictures will start to look like
<u>one</u> *animated* picture.

Don't forget to
add your own sound-effects!

LEFT HAND HERE

GEORGE PINS
A PREDATOR

79

RIGHT
THUMB
HERE

GEORGE PINS
A PREDATOR

FLIP-O-RAMA 2

(pages 83 and 85)

Remember, flip *only* page 83.
While you are flipping, be sure you
can see the picture on page 83
and the one on page 85.
If you flip quickly, the two
pictures will start to look like
<u>one</u> *animated* picture.

Don't forget to
add your own sound-effects!

LEFT HAND HERE

HAROLD BONKS
A BAD GUY

83

HAROLD BONKS
A BAD GUY

FLIP-O-RAMA 3

(pages 87 and 89)

Remember, flip *only* page 87.
While you are flipping, be sure you
can see the picture on page 87
and the one on page 89.
If you flip quickly, the two
pictures will start to look like
<u>one</u> *animated* picture.

Don't forget to
add your own sound-effects!

LEFT HAND HERE

GEORGE AND HAROLD
SAVE THE DAY
(FOR NOW)

87

RIGHT
THUMB
HERE

88

GEORGE AND HAROLD
SAVE THE DAY
(FOR NOW)

90

CHAPTER 16

THE ASSAULT OF THE EQUALLY EVIL LUNCHROOM ZOMBIE NERDS

George and Harold had barely caught their breath when Captain Underpants finally showed up.

"Tra-La-Laaaaa!" he said. "I'm here to fight for Truth, Justice, and *all* that is Pre-Shrunk and Cottony!"

"Where were you back in chapter fifteen when we needed you?" asked George.

"I was at the shoe shop ordering a cheeseburger," said Captain Underpants.

While our three heroes were talking, nobody noticed that Zorx, Klax, and Jennifer had slithered away. The wounded space guys approached the lunchroom loudspeakers and called for their evil zombie nerds.

"Zombie Nerds!" instructed Jennifer. "Destroy Captain Underpants – and his little friends, too!"

Soon, every evil zombie nerd in the entire school put down their *Omni* magazines and headed for the cafeteria.

"Must destroy Underpants," they
groaned. *"Must destroy Underpants!"*

Suddenly, our three heroes were
surrounded by evil, vicious zombie nerds.
Closer and closer they came.

"Oh, no!" cried George. "What do we do
now?"

"To the Underwear Cave!" shouted
Captain Underpants.

"There *is* no *Underwear Cave*!" said
Harold.

"Really?" said Captain Underpants. "Well,
let's just climb up that ladder instead."

George, Harold, and Captain Underpants scurried up the ladder, and soon they were all on the roof.

"Well, we're safe now," said Harold.

"Yep," said George.

"That's for sure," said Captain Underpants.

CHAPTER 17
OH YEAH?

It didn't take long before George, Harold, and Captain Underpants looked behind them.

"Hey," said Harold. "What's that big spaceship thingy doing on the roof of the school?"

"And where did that *super evil rapidly growing* dandelion come from?" asked Captain Underpants.

George and Harold gasped. They looked at each other with the sudden panicked realization that only children who have accidentally created a giant mutated garden nuisance would know.

"Er…" stammered George. "We have *no idea* how *that* happened."

"Er… *Yeah*," said Harold. "Absolutely *no idea* at all!"

At that moment, the door to the roof swung open. Zorx poked his evil head out and shouted, "We've got you now!"

With nowhere else to run, our three heroes quickly scurried up the ladder of the big spaceship thingy and closed the door behind them.

Inside the spaceship, George, Harold, and Captain Underpants discovered a refrigerator filled with strange juices.

"Look," said George. "Here's a carton of ANTI-EVIL-ZOMBIE-NERD JUICE. How convenient!"

"And look at this," said Harold. "A carton of ULTRA NASTY SELF-DESTRUCT JUICE. Now *this* could come in handy!"

"And look what I've found," said Captain Underpants. "A whole carton of EXTRA-STRENGTH SUPER POWER JUICE!"

"Hey, gimme that!" said George, snapping the carton out of Captain Underpants's hands.

98

CHAPTER 18

SPACE SLAVES

Suddenly, the door of the spaceship swung open, and the three evil space guys slithered inside.

"Step away from the refrigerator!" screamed Jennifer. "And get into that jail cell!"

George and Harold hid their juice cartons behind their backs, and our three heroes stepped quickly into the jail cell.

Zorx started up the engines and the spaceship lifted off. It rose a hundred metres in the air and hovered over the school.

"You three puny earthlings are very fortunate," said Jennifer. "You will get to witness the destruction of your planet from the safety of your jail cell. Afterwards, you will have the honour of being our obedient space slaves!"

"Aw, *man!*" said George and Harold.

"Quickly, Klax," said Jennifer. "Get me a carton of SUPER EVIL RAPID-GROWTH JUICE from the refrigerator. We can pour it into our spray gun and shower it upon our evil zombie nerds!"

100

CHAPTER 19

THE BIG SWITCHEROO

Klax returned with a carton of SUPER EVIL
RAPID-GROWTH JUICE, and placed it on the
control panel.

"*Soon*," said Jennifer, "Earth will be
OURS!"

The three aliens threw back their heads
and laughed and laughed.

Suddenly, George got an idea.

He whispered to Harold for a second or two, then he quietly reached through the bars of the jail cell and swiped Klax's carton of SUPER EVIL RAPID-GROWTH JUICE.

George carefully peeled the label off the carton, and stuck it over the label of his Ultra Nasty Self-Destruct Juice.

While he was busy doing that, Harold reached through the bars and switched the labels of the SPRAY GUN and the FUEL TANK.

Finally, George reached back through the bars and put his carton of ULTRA NASTY SELF-DESTRUCT JUICE (which now read SUPER EVIL RAPID-GROWTH JUICE) on the control panel.

"I don't get it," whispered Captain Underpants. "The fuel tank now says SPRAY GUN, and the spray gun now says FUEL TANK, and the rapid-growth juice has been replaced with self-destruct juice… What's it all mean?"

"You'll find out," said Harold, sadly.

When the three evil space guys had finished laughing triumphantly, Jennifer reached for the carton that read SUPER EVIL RAPID-GROWTH JUICE and poured it into the nozzle that read SPRAY GUN.

"Oh, I get it," said Captain Underpants. "That space guy didn't pour growth juice into the spray gun – he poured self-destruct juice into the *fuel tank*!"

"Yep," George said sadly.

"And that means this spaceship thingy is going to explode into millions of pieces!"

"Right," said Harold gloomily.

The spaceship began to sputter and shake as smoke billowed out of the control panels. Soon sparks were flying and ceiling tiles were falling.

Captain Underpants smiled proudly because he had figured out George's plan. But his smile didn't last long.

"Hey," he cried. "*WE'RE* in the space-ship thingy! What's gonna happen to *us*?"

"We had to sacrifice ourselves to save the world," said George. "I'm afraid we're not going to make it."

"*Of course* we'll make it," cried Captain Underpants. "We've got *Wedgie Power* on our side!"

CHAPTER 20

THE GREAT ESCAPE

Captain Underpants grabbed a roll of toilet paper from the jail cell lavatory.

"We can swing to safety on *this*!" he said.

"You can't *swing* on toilet paper," said Harold.

"Sure I can," said Captain Underpants. "I did it in my last comic book!"

Captain Underpants opened the jail cell window and tossed the toilet paper into a tall tree below them. "Come on, fellas," he said. "Let's swing out of here before this spaceship explodes!"

"That toilet paper won't hold you," said George. "It's not strong enough!"

"Sure it is," said Captain Underpants. "It's *two-ply*!"

George and Harold grabbed Captain Underpants's cape. "Don't jump!" they cried.

But Captain Underpants wouldn't listen. He jumped out the window with George and Harold still clinging to his cape.

"AAAAAAAAAAAAAAHGH!" they screamed as they fell to the ground and were killed instantly.

Just kidding.

Of course, the toilet paper could not support the weight of our three heroes, and for a moment, it looked like they were doomed.

But suddenly, Captain Underpants's red polyester cape opened up like a parachute — *PHOOOOP!*

George, Harold, and the Waistband Warrior floated down safely as the spaceship above them exploded.

KA-BOOM!

"Hallelujah!" cried Harold. *"We're not gonna die!* WE'RE NOT GONNA DIE!"

"Or…" said George. "Maybe we *are*."

CHAPTER 21

THE DELIRIOUSLY DANGEROUS DEATH-DEFYING DANDELION OF DOOM

George, Harold, and Captain Underpants floated downwards, directly into the waiting jaws of the Dandelion of Doom.

"Aw, *man!*" cried Harold. "We *could* have got killed in a cool exploding spaceship. But instead, we're gonna get eaten by a *dandelion*. How *humiliating!*"

"Yeah," George moaned. "People are going to be giggling at our funerals."

The dandelion munched Captain Underpants and swung George and Harold around like a couple of rag dolls.

The two boys flew off and landed on the roof of the school.

"HELP MEEEeeEEEEeeEEEeeeEEE," screamed Captain Underpants as the Dandelion of Doom swung him back and forth.

"What should we do?" cried Harold.

"I've got an idea," said George. "It's a bad idea, and I know we're going to regret it, but we've got to act fast! The fate of the entire planet is in our hands."

The next time the giant evil dandelion lurched toward the boys, George poured some EXTRA-STRENGTH SUPER POWER JUICE into Captain Underpants's mouth.

"What do you think is going to happen now?" asked Harold.

"I don't know," said George. "But I have a feeling it's gonna involve incredibly graphic violence!"

CHAPTER 22

THE INCREDIBLY GRAPHIC VIOLENCE CHAPTER, PART 2 (IN FLIP-O-RAMA™)

WARNING:

The following chapter contains scenes of a very unpleasant nature.

All nastiness was performed by a qualified stuntman and a licensed stuntplant. Do not attempt to battle giant evil dandelions at home, even if you have recently consumed EXTRA-STRENGTH SUPER POWER JUICE.

Such behaviour could result in serious boo-boos.

—The National Board of Boo-Boo Prevention

FLIP-O-RAMA 4

(pages 119 and 121)

Remember, flip *only* page 119.
While you are flipping, be sure you
can see the picture on page 119
and the one on page 121.
If you flip quickly, the two
pictures will start to look like
<u>one</u> *animated* picture.

Don't forget to
add your own sound-effects!

LEFT HAND HERE

WHEN DANDELIONS
ATTACK

119

RIGHT
THUMB
HERE

RIGHT
INDEX
FINGER
HERE

120

WHEN DANDELIONS ATTACK

FLIP-O-RAMA 5

(pages 123 and 125)

Remember, flip *only* page 123.
While you are flipping, be sure you
can see the picture on page 123
and the one on page 125.
If you flip quickly, the two
pictures will start to look like
<u>one</u> *animated* picture.

Don't forget to
add your own sound-effects!

LEFT HAND HERE

THE WEDGIE WEED WHACKER

123

RIGHT
THUMB
HERE

THE WEDGIE WEED
WHACKER

125

FLIP-O-RAMA 6

(pages 127 and 129)

Remember, flip *only* page 127.
While you are flipping, be sure you
can see the picture on page 127
and the one on page 129.
If you flip quickly, the two
pictures will start to look like
<u>one</u> *animated* picture.

Don't forget to
add your own sound-effects!

LEFT HAND HERE

HOORAY FOR CAPTAIN UNDERPANTS!

127

RIGHT
THUMB
HERE

128

HOORAY FOR CAPTAIN UNDERPANTS!

CHAPTER 23

THE TWENTY-THIRD CHAPTER

Captain Underpants (with the help of his newly developed super powers) had defeated the deliriously dangerous death-defying Dandelion of Doom! Now, the only thing left to do was to stop the evil zombie nerds.

"Oh, *HOW* are we going to conquer the evil zombie nerds?" asked George. "How will we ever change them back to normal?"

"Well, we could try this A<small>NTI</small>-E<small>VIL</small>-
Z<small>OMBIE</small>-N<small>ERD</small> J<small>UICE</small>," said Harold.

George rolled his eyes. "I was hoping
for something a *little* more dramatic," he
said, "but we're running out of pages. Let's
do it."

So Harold mixed up a batch of ANTI-EVIL-ZOMBIE-NERD ROOT BEER, and ordered everybody in the school to drink some.

The evil zombie nerds lined up. "Must drink root beer," they moaned. "Must drink root beer."

When the last zombie nerd had
swallowed his last sip of root beer, George
ordered Captain Underpants to get dressed
back up like Mr Krupp.

"But I'll lose my super powers if I put
on clothing," said Captain Underpants.
"The power of underwear must be —"

"Just put the clothes on!" George
instructed.

Captain Underpants did as he was told,
and then George poured water over the
hero's head.

"Now all we can do is wait," said Harold.
"Wait and hope that everybody returns to
normal."

CHAPTER 24

TO MAKE A LONG STORY SHORT

They did.

CHAPTER 25

BACK TO NORMAL?

"Hooray," said Harold. "It's great to have everybody back to normal."

"Yep," said George. "That's for sure."

But "back to normal" probably wasn't the best choice of words. For while the students and faculty were the same as they'd always been, something had definitely *changed* about Mr. Krupp.

Because from that day on, whenever he heard the sounds of fingers snapping...

SNAP!

...Mr. Krupp not only turned back into "you-know-who," but he also had *Extra-Strength Super Powers*.

And if you thought it was hard for George and Harold to keep up with him *before*, well...

…you ain't seen nothin' yet!

"OH, NO!" screamed Harold.

"HERE WE GO AGAIN!" screamed George.

CD-ROM SYSTEM REQUIREMENTS

WINDOWS®

- Pentium® 233 MHz processor
- Windows® 98/Me/2000/XP
- 128 MB RAM
- Windows® compatible sound card and speakers
- 640x480 resolution color display
- 4X speed multi-session CD-ROM drive or CD-RW/DVD-ROM drive
- Mouse
- Minimum browser requirements: Safari™ 1.0, Microsoft Internet Explorer® 3.x, Netscape Navigator® 3.x

MACINTOSH®

- 400 MHz PowerPC® processor
- System 10 (OSX)
- 128 MB RAM
- 640x480 resolution color display
- 4X speed multi-session CD-ROM drive or CD-RW/DVD-ROM drive
- Mouse
- Minimum browser requirements: Safari™ 1.0, Microsoft Internet Explorer® 3.x, Netscape Navigator® 3.x